The Rich Culture and History of Kyrgyzstan

The Rich Culture and History of Kyrgyzstan

ASKAR BESHIMOV
DR. GAURAV GUPTA

PRABHAT
PRAKASHAN

Published by
PRABHAT PRAKASHAN PVT. LTD.
4/19 Asaf Ali Road,
New Delhi-110 002 (INDIA)
e-mail: prabhatbooks@gmail.com

ISBN 978-93-5562-431-4
THE RICH CULTURE AND HISTORY OF KYRGYZSTAN
by Askar Beshimov and Dr. Gaurav Gupta

Edition
First, 2024

Price
₹ 300 (Rupees Three Hundred Only)

Printed at
Japan Art, Delhi

Author's Note

In the heart of Central Asia lies a land of enchanting landscapes, vibrant traditions, and a history that stretches back millennia. Kyrgyzstan, a country nestled between rugged mountain ranges, has long been a place of mystery and intrigue. The pages that follow aim to unravel the rich tapestry that has been woven by countless generations of resilient and creative people.

Its history is a testament to the human spirit's indomitable nature. From the ancient Scythians who roamed the steppes to the Silk Road caravans that traversed its valleys, this land has always been a crossroads of cultures and a witness to the ebb and flow of history. The chapters that delve into the past will transport you through time, from the mighty Kyrgyz Khanate to the Soviet era and the path to independence. It is a history marked by challenges, conquests, and a constant quest for identity.

The culture of this country is a kaleidoscope of traditions, art, and a unique way of life. The nomadic heritage of the

Kyrgyz people, their love for music, their equestrian skills, and their warm hospitality; all paint a vivid picture of this nation's soul. In this book, you will explore the intricacies of Kyrgyz cuisine, experience the beauty of yurts, and gain insights into the customs that have sustained communities through generations.

Its breathtaking landscapes are some of the world's best-kept secrets. From the snow-capped peaks of the Tien Shan and Pamir mountain ranges to the serene beauty of Issyk-Kul Lake, the country is a sanctuary for nature enthusiasts. This book will take you on a visual tour through these landscapes, celebrating the pristine wilderness, rare wildlife, and the role of the natural world in shaping Kyrgyz culture.

"The Rich Culture and History of Kyrgyzstan" is a labor of love, a tribute to a land that has enriched our lives and, I hope, will enrich yours too. Whether you're a seasoned traveler, a scholar, or someone simply curious about this far-off land, Kyrgyzstan has something to offer. The stories and insights shared in this book are meant to be an invitation to embark on your own journey of discovery, to explore this land, meet its people, and find your own connection to its history and culture.

❑

KYRGYZ REPUBLIC (COUNTRY PROFILE)

The Kyrgyz Republic (or Kyrgyzstan) is located in the northeastern part of Central Asia, occupies the western part of the Tien Shan Mountain system and the northern mountainous regions of the Pamir-Alai. More than 80% of the republic's territory is located at an altitude of more than 1,500 meters above sea level.

It has borders with Kazakhstan, Uzbekistan, Tajikistan and the People's Republic of China.

Kyrgyzstan consists of 9 administrative-territorial units - Chui region, Talas region, Issyk-Kul region, Naryn region, Jalal-Abad region, Osh region, Batken region and 2 main cities – Bishkek and Osh. Regional centres - Talas, Karakol, Naryn, Jalal-Abad, Osh, Batken.

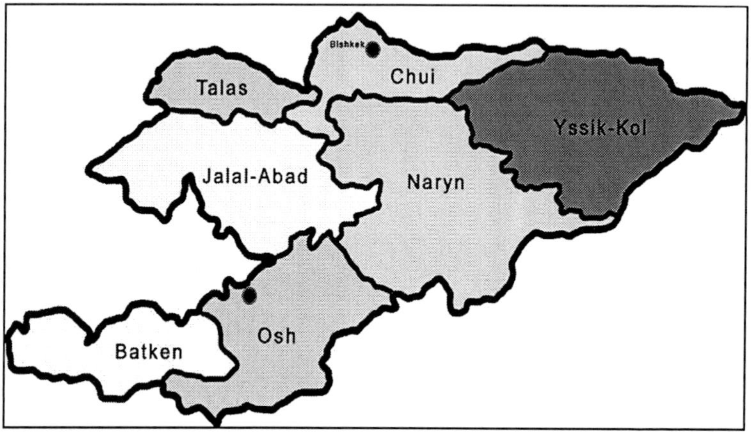

Kyrgyz Republic declared its independence on August 31, 1991 (USSR). Population is 7 million people. There are more than 100 ethnic groups live in the country.

- **Capital:** Bishkek
- **Area:** 199,9 thousand sq km
- **Languages:** Kyrgyz is its state language, Russian is the official language.
- **Currency:** Kyrgyz som (KGC, code 417)

- **Internet domen:** .kg
- **Telephone code:** +996
- **Life expectancy:** 67 years (men) 76 years (women)

State Symbols

Flag **National Emblem**

The Flag features of yellow Tunduk inside of the 40 rays of sun on the red ground.

The Emblem features a hawk beating wings in from of the Tien-Shan Mountains, Issyk-Kul Lake and rising sun. With wheat and cotton covered round with the sigh The Kyrgyz Republic.

Politics

According to the Constitution, the Kyrgyz Republic (Kyrgyzstan) is an independent, sovereign, democratic, unitary, legal, secular and social state.

The Head of the state is the President, elected for five years and no more than two terms. The President is the head of the executive power. Presidential elections took place on January 10, 2021, which were won by the Prime Minister of the Kyrgyz Republic Sadyr Nurgozhoevich Zhaparov. On January 28, 2021, he was inaugurated.

President: Sadyr Zhaparov

The highest executive body is the Cabinet of Ministers, headed by the Chairman. Since October 13, 2021, this post has been held by Akylbek Zhaparov (at the same time he is the Head of the Administration of the President of the Kyrgyz Republic).

Jogorku Kenesh – is the Parliament of the Kyrgyz Republic, consists of 90 deputies and is elected for a term of 5 years. Toraga/Speaker of Parliament Nurlanbek Shakiev.

Juridical system – Supreme Court, Local Courts and Chief Prosecutor.

History

Kyrgyz Republic has history of more than 2000 years. The modern territory of the country was geographically isolated by high mountains, that helped to keep its ancient culture of nomads. Scythians (Scyth, Saka) were the first inhabitants of the modern territory of Kyrgyzstan.

At the middle of IX century on the ruins of Uyghur Khaganate, there was upraise of Kyrgyz tribes, joined into Kyrgyz Khaganate, strong and rich Khanate with big territory from Guligani (Baikal) till Tibet, whole territory of Gelolu (Seven rivers) modern Central Asia territory. They had strong political structure – with Ajo at the head (Kagan or Khan) with 20 Beks (Ministers) and 15 clerks for clerical work, taxes, finance and law. By the end of Kyrgyz Khaganate, era of Turkic domination at Eurasia changed by domination of Mongol tribes. Kyrgyz tribes were overrun by Mongols, Qing Dynasty and Kokand Khanate. At the end of 19th century Russian Empire came to Kyrgyz land. At 1936 was established Kyrgyz Soviet Socialistic Republic and became part of the Soviet Union. During that period was changes in cultural, educational and social life. Due to the political changes at USSR and strong believe to be independent state, the Kyrgyz Republic declared independence from the Soviet Union at 31st of August 1991, when the new history of Independent Kyrgyzstan started.

Population

Population of the Kyrgyz Republic is 7 million (2022). This population is equivalent to 0.08% total world population and ranks number 111 in the list of countries by population. The population density in Kyrgyzstan is 32 per km2.

Total land area is 199,9 thousand km2. 35,6% of population is urban. The median age in Kyrgyzstan is 25,5 years. The largest ethnic group is Kyrgyz – 73,3%. Other big ethnic groups are Uzbek - 14,7%, Russian - 5,5%, others – 6,4%. There are over 100 ethnicities in Kyrgyzstan - Dungans, Uygurs, Tajiks, Kazakh, Ukrainians, Kurds and Germans, etc. Islam is a dominant religion of the Kyrgyzstan - Muslim 75%, Russian Orthodox 20%, other 5%.

Multinational population of Kyrgyzstan is a richness of the country, with different cultures, languages, confession and background, nevertheless today they are united in one country, being the smalt of the mosaic.

Currency

The Kyrgyz Som (KGS) is an official national currency. It divides into 100 tyiyn (coins). Banknotes are in denomination 20, 50, 100, 200, 500, 1000, 2000, 5000. Coins are in denomination of 1, 3, 5 and 10 soms. The 1 som is the smallest unit of the national currency. Every banknote bill had a features of famous people portraits, main geographical and heritage sites, architects and musical instruments. Kyrgyzstan is mostly cash based- economy. But now possible to find in ever town and big village ATM Machines with possibility to withdraw from Visa Card, Master Card, etc. Banks and exchange offices could be found in every town and village. National Bank officially fixed the exchanges rates. http://www.nbkr.kg/

Language

Main state language is Kyrgyz (Turkic language of Kipchak branch) from 1991. In 1997 Russian language was adopted as an official language. Kyrgyz written in the Arabic alphabet until the 20th century. In Latin scripts was written from 1928 till 1941. From that period Kyrgyz language is in Cyrillic script. According to the last data's 4,1 million people spoke Kyrgyz and more than 2,5 million spoke Russian.

Capital

Bishkek is the capital of the Kyrgyz Republic. Its political, economic and cultural centre. Bishkek located at Chuy region, at the slopes of the Kyrgyz Range, at about 700-900 meters above sea level. Total territory of the city is 127 km2, territory with nearby villages and areas is about 200 km2. Total population of the town is about 1,000,000 people.

The capital Bishkek and the Kyrgyz Ala-Too mountains

Bishkek History

First archaeological signs dated from V-IV c. BC were found at the current territory of Bishkek town. Chui valley was advantageous and favourable stop on the Great Silk

Road. Ancient settlement of Djiul (VII-XII centuries) was located at the Northern part of the town, till our days' people call it Kuznechnaya krepost – "forge fortress", because of the densely populated area of handicrafts, artisans and merchants. In 1825 there was settlement of Pishpek, organized by Madali Khan from Kokand Khanid. Two times Pishpek citadel attacked and destroyed by Russian troops. Later on, there was organized bazaar and settlement, at 1878 Pishpek became town. In 1924 here arrived Check and Slovak cooperative "Interghelpo", they built up town and Pishpek became administrative center of Kyrgyz Autonomic Country. In 1926 town renamed into Frunze, named after Mikhail Vasilievich Frunze – revolutionary, soviet military and statesman, head of Red Army of the Soviets. In 1936 – Frunze is a capital of Kyrgyz Soviet Republic. In 1991 after the Independence city was renamed to its historical name Bishkek.

Cultural life in Kyrgyzstan

Though Kyrgyzstan might not be known as a centre for performing arts, there are actually a number of famous writers and performers from the region. There is a thriving arts scene in Kyrgyzstan, with theatres and arts schools around the country. Students can study dance, performance, music and filmmaking, and there are performance spaces that regularly host productions.

The State Kyrgyz Opera and Ballet Theatre was founded in 1926 as a training theatre. The current building was built in 1955, and still holds regular performances to this day.

Museums in Kyrgyzstan

The State Historical Museum and the Museum of Fine Arts in Bishkek are two of the largest and most famous museums in Kyrgyzstan, but a trip to Bishkek would be incomplete without visiting the Frunze House Museum, where visitors can enter his perfectly preserved house. The Osh State Historical and Archaeological Museum showcases the only UNESCO World Heritage Site completely in Kyrgyzstan, while the Przewalski House Museum in Karakol is a tribute to the famous explorer, one of the first to map the area. Next to Burana Tower is an archaeological museum, where visitors can learn more about the ancient history of Kyrgyzstan.

Monuments, Memorials in Kyrgyzstan

Some monuments and memorials in Kyrgyzstan remain from Soviet times, while others have only appeared since independence. New statues of Manas and older statues of Lenin dot the country, while monuments to other notable figures (such as Chingiz Aitmatov, Toktogul Satylganov, and Przewalski) can also be found. In Bishkek, there are also monuments to those who died in the Second World War (at Victory Square), and a Memorial to Those Who Died for Freedom (commemorating those killed in the 2010 revolution). Ata-Beyit, close to Bishkek, is a memorial complex located near a mass grave where political prisoners had been executed, and serves as a memorial to those who died during the political purges.

The Epic of Manas is a great masterpiece of folklore of Kyrgyz people

The Epic of Manas is perhaps the most famous part of Kyrgyz culture, and is the longest epic poem in the world.

At 20 times longer than the Odyssey, this epic tells the life of Manas, an epic warrior, and his son and grandson. The original tale was passed orally from performer to performer, who were known as manaschi. The tale was written down starting in the 1800s, and the first complete version was published in the 1920s. The Epic of Manas has since been translated into many different languages, and published in the Soviet Union and abroad.

In one of its iterations, it consists of more than 500 000 lines. In 1995 people of Kyrgyzstan celebrated the 1,000th anniversary of the Epic of Manas.

Throughout the ages the Epic of Manas went the round, enriching and getting new shades, but keeping a clear storyline. True skill of the narrative work was achieved by national storytellers called manaschy. They can tell fascinating stories about the great hero Manas and his exploits for many hours. Each manaschy has his own style of presentation and his own interpretation of the events of the epic, but all of them keep to the same storyline. Currently 35 different iterations of the epic are known. They were written from the words the famous and skilful narrators S.Orozbakov, S.Karalaev, Togolok Moldo and others.

The main character of the epic is the hero Manas who united Kyrgyz people in the struggle for independence. By the way, the main idea of the epic is closely connected with the pursuit of independence, consolidation and prosperity of the nation. The epic poem consists of three parts that reflect the lives of the people in three generations. The first part talks about Manas and the fight for his motherland. The second part is devoted to his son Semetei and his exploits. iI the third part of the epic the plot is built around Manas's grandson Seitek and his efforts to unite the people.

The Epic of Manas is not only the greatest work of national folklore, but also a storehouse of knowledge about the life of Kyrgyz people of that period (9th-10th centuries). It describes all aspects of people's life, economy, customs and traditions. It provides information on the ethnic composition of the population and the neighbouring peoples, their politics and economy. According to the epic is you can also understand people's conceptions of geography, religion, medicine, and philosophy. The famous researcher Ch.Valikhanov even said that the Epic of Manas was the real encyclopaedia of Kyrgyz people.

Kyrgyzstan Literature

Kyrgyzstan's literature extends across centuries, though it wasn't always written down. Since very little of the population was literate until relatively recently, many poets (known as akyns) travelled from village to village performing their works. Some works, like the Epic of Manas, were memorized and passed down orally between generations of performers, known as manaschi. Literacy increased under the Soviet Union, when schooling became more common, and not just part of a religious education. Starting in the 20th century, writers, poets, and linguists flourished, producing excellent works that became famous around the world.

The writer and thinker Chingiz Aitmatov

Chingiz Aitmatov is revered for building a bridge between the world of traditional Kyrgyz folklore and modern Eurasian literature. His writings illuminate the challenges that faced the peoples of the Soviet Union both before and after its demise, and his own life is an integral part of that broader turbulent pattern.

He was born on December 12, 1928, and brought up in the village of Sheker in the Talas region of northern Kyrgyzstan. He studied in Jambul (in present-day Kazakhstan), Frunze (now Bishkek), and Moscow (Russia).

Chingiz Aitmatov was equally respected inside and outside the USSR: He received India's Jawaharlal Nehru award, and was named a member of the World Academy of Science and Arts and the European Academy of Science, Arts, and Literature. His works were translated into more than 170 languages and sold more than 60 million copies worldwide.

In October 1986, Aitmatov founded the famous Issyk-Kul Forum, which brought intellectuals from the Soviet bloc and the West together at a lakeside resort to discuss major global challenges face to face. He served as Kyrgyz Ambassador to UNESCO, EU, NATO, and the Benelux countries.

Throughout his life, Chingiz Aitmatov preserved his love for his fellow men, and for nature and the animal world. His last novel, titled "When the Mountains Fall Down: The Eternal Bride," was written in 2005 as a final appeal to his people to preserve the beauty of the Celestial Mountains (Tengir-Too in Kyrgyz, Tian-Shan in Chinese), which the Kyrgyz have traditionally regarded as sacred. The two heroes of the novel, a journalist named Arsen Samanchin and an indigenous snow leopard (Jaa Bars), both become victims of international poaching in a tale of the perils of the greedy and careless exploitation of the environment.

Sports in Kyrgyzstan

Sports in Kyrgyzstan are more than just recreation; they're training for life. People needed to be strong and resourceful to survive in the mountains and steppes, and sports helped them gain the strength and skills necessary. Sports also reflect the traditions and values of the Kyrgyz people, and helped them pass on their culture from one generation to another.

The most famous of the sports in Kyrgyzstan are horse games. Kok-boru features two teams of riders fighting for possession of a dead sheep, which they must land in a goal to score points.

Wrestling is another popular sport in Kyrgyzstan. Here, the connection between sport and survival is a little clearer - strength and agility would be useful in a variety of situations.

Hunting competitions helped hone the skills of animals, like birds and dogs. Birds of prey can be trained as hunting aids, but are never fully domesticated.

Intellectual games build a player's capacity to think strategically. Ordo, a game that involves throwing vertebrae in order to hit a target at the center of a circle.

Kyrgyzstan Ancient Culture and Traditions

Kyrgyzstan culture is heavily influenced by the traditions from nomadic life. Kyrgyz culture features influence from Russia, Persia, and Turkey, but yet remains something entirely unique. Nature influences are prominent, from the designs to the music, and many traditions reflect the fact that nomads lived closely with nature. Perhaps the most well-known aspect of Kyrgyz culture is the Epic of Manas, an incredibly long poem passed down orally for generations.

As nomads, the Kyrgyz people always lived closely with nature. From their housing to their clothing, everything was designed to adapt to changing weather and locations. Yurts are easy to take apart and carry, and can be made warmer for winter, and cooler for summer. The textiles inside of yurts, such as shyrdaks and tush kyiz (felt rugs and embroidered hangings), take their inspiration from designs found in nature, such as plants, animals, and landscapes. Even clothing was made out of natural materials, and designed to be comfortable while still stylish.

Horses were, and still are, central to Kyrgyzstan culture. They provided not only transportation, but played crucial roles in wars and even cuisine. Kumis, or kymyz, is made from mare's milk, and some traditional dishes feature horse meat. Horses traditionally played roles in courtship and marriage ceremonies, and could be used as payment or as dowries. Some instruments were even designed so that they could be played on horseback, and the beat of hooves can be heard in traditional Kyrgyz music.

It's no surprise then that horsemanship is valued in Kyrgyz culture. Sports are ways to develop both riders and horses, and to make both better prepared for hunting and battle. Competitions testing dogs and birds of prey on their speed and accuracy found the best hunters, who would be essential in the winter.

Many of these elements can still be found today, though Kyrgyzstan is also still a modern country. People are proud of the culture in Kyrgyzstan, and events are held to make sure that it is kept alive and promoted. Visitors can expect to be immersed in these nomadic and traditional elements, especially if they stay with a host family.

Kyrgyz Yurts

Yurts are one of the most essential parts of Kyrgyz culture, and are more than just houses. They represent the family, the earth, and the universe, and cover everything from birth to death. Yurts hold much of Kyrgyz culture, from important rituals and ceremonies, to craftsmanship and traditional artistry.

The basis of the wooden frame of a yurt is composed of several elements. The setting of a yurt begins with the doorway "bosogo", usually facing south or south-east. The walls are a grid of birch poles called "kerege". The base of a dome is also assembled of poles called "uuk", then goes a rim called "tyundyuk". Tyundyuk is used for entry of sunlight into the yurt as well as for going out of smoke. Tyundyuk is one of the most recognizable symbols of Kyrgyzstan, which is represented on the flag of the country. Outside yurt is covered with woven straw called "chiy" and thick felt "kiyiz". The doorway is also covered with felt, or there stand double doors instead.

In the center of the yurt there is a hearth called "kolomto". The back of the yurt is called "dzhyuk". There you can usually see chests and folded blankets, pillows and carpets. Between kolomto and dzhyuk there is the place of honor called "ter", where sits the head of the family or the most distinguished guests.

The right side of the yurt ("epchi jak") is the female half, which holds stocks of food, dishes, various items needed in the household. The left side of the yurt is called "er jak", the male half. There are a saddle, harness, weapons, animal skins. The floor and walls of a yurt are decorated with beautiful patterned rugs called "shyrdaks".

Kyrgyz Textiles

Kyrgyz textiles feature mostly designs from nature, and materials that were easily found in the mountains and their surroundings. Felt and wool are common materials, as are reeds and embroidery thread. Most of the motifs and designs reflect the mountains, rivers, plants, and animals that live in Kyrgyzstan.

Shyrdaks are the most iconic Kyrgyz textile, easily recognizable from their bold patterns.

Tush kyiz are intricate embroideries, often made for marriages. The designs feature plants and flowers, and sometimes animals, embroidered onto a soft cloth, and are hung on the walls of yurts.

Kurak are items sewn together from fabric scraps. The name kurak comes from the word "kura", which means sewn together, or put together from separate pieces. Kurak may be hats, children's clothing, blankets for cradles, wedding curtains, mattresses, pillows, covers for saddles, bags, or carpets.

Ala kyiz are also made of felt, and may feature similar designs as shyrdaks, but are made through a different process.

Chiy are reeds that grow on the steppes, and are harvested and dried to make mats.

Kyrgyz Music

Kyrgyz music is most famous for how evocative it is of nature and life in the mountains. Many songs have lyrics about the nomadic lifestyle, but even without words, the music reflects the sounds and feelings of not only the landscape, but of the experiences essential to living there. There are a variety of instruments in Kyrgyzstan, all of which can be played in ensembles or separately.

Since ancient time music played an important role in the life of Kyrgyz people. Any holiday in the village did not do without music, and young and old people gathered to listen to wonderful tunes of master musicians. Kyrgyz people, like any nation, have their traditional musical instruments, reflecting the unique national character.

The most widely used instrument is komuz. It is made by skilled craftsmen from a single piece of wood (usually juniper, apricot or walnut). Its length does not exceed 80-90 cm. Komuz has three strings. It is usually played while sitting: A musician is keeping the instrument in a horizontal position, the left hand is holding the strings on the neck, and fingers of the right hand are running over them. Komuz can be tuned up in different ways. Musicians can play cheerful and sonorous melodies and lyrical motives, taking the soul as well.

Another well-known musical symbol of Kyrgyz people is temir-komuz, an oral stringed musical instrument of arched shape. The fact that it is made of metal reflects its title (temir in translation from Kyrgyz means “iron”). The sound emitted by this musical instrument is unusual, but it is very soft and charming. Women and children often play the temir-komuz.

Kyl-kyak is a bow musical instrument with two strings. It is made of juniper or apricot tree wood, strings and bow are made of the finest horse hair. Musicians play on kyl-kyak, holding it upright on the lap and moving the bow. . The sound of this music is quite specific. It’s hollow, but in some ways resembles the tone of the human voice.

Chopo-chor is a kind of wind instrument made of clay. It was popular mainly in the southern agricultural regions of the country. It is an elongated tube with openings which are periodically covered with fingers during the process of playing it.

National drum is called dobulbash. It has a diameter of about 30 cm, and covered with camel skin on the top. It gives very sonorous rhythmic sound that can be helpful during military campaigns or magic rituals.

As you can see, all national instruments are made of materials and items that are available in a nomadic household. This gives musical instruments unique flavor and spirit of nomadic freedom.

Kyrgyz National Clothing

Kyrgyz clothing reflects the lifestyle and regions of Kyrgyzstan, with designs and materials drawn from nomadic life. Wool, felt, leather, skins, and coarse cloth

are the main materials used for Kyrgyz clothing, with ornamentation taken from tribal traditions and nature. Even though many people wear Western clothing, traditional elements are still visible everywhere, and people are proud of their traditional clothing in Kyrgyzstan.

Features of the nomadic lifestyle of Kyrgyz people have been reflected in their national clothes. First, the clothes had to be light and comfortable, so that a nomad could comfortably ride on horseback. Second, the clothes had to be strong, but uncomplicated, so that it could be home-made. Third, it must reliably protect people from the cold, that is important in a mountain climate. The main materials for making clothes were coarse wool, felt, fur and leather. The noble families could afford expensive clothes made of fabrics from the towns of the Great Silk Road.

The outerwear is called “chapan”. The chapan is a kind of padded coat made of a strong and warm woollen fabric, with buttons and high collar. In winter nomads wore sheepskin coat named “ton” and fur coats “ichiks” made of fox fur, wolf or lynx. The main traditional shoes are boots decorated with colourful ornaments, with long tops and narrow toes.

Men wore wide trousers made of leather or suede, embroidered with colored threads (“chalbar”, “kandagay”), shirts (“keynek”) and felt robe (“kementay”). Noble and rich people wore jewelry. A male attribute of wealth in the clothing was a wide leather belt (kemer), decorated with various silver incuts.

The traditional women's clothing consisted of long white shirts or dresses ("keynek") and long pantaloons. Young women wore sleeveless jackets of coloured velvet ("chyptama"). Married women wore skirts with fur and patterned embroidery ("beldemchi").

Headwear always played a special role in Kyrgyz traditional clothing. Ak kalpak is a white felt hat worn by men. It is one of the important symbols of Kyrgyz people. The hat in the shape of a turban made of fine white muslin is called "elechek". Traditionally it is worn by married women.

National Cuisine

National cuisine in Kyrgyzstan is especially rich and diverse. It has been developed throughout the history of

Kyrgyz people and collected the most delicious dishes and beverages from the period of nomadic life, and dishes of neighbouring nations in the region as well.

As the nomadic lifestyle required a lot of strength and energy, the national dishes of Kyrgyz people had extraordinary nutritional and caloric content. Their main ingredients were meat, milk, flour and cereals.

Most traditional dishes don't do without meat. Kyrgyz people like to eat lamb, beef, yak meat, and especially horse meat. The most famous dish is the Kyrgyz beshbarmak. It is boiled chopped lamb with onions and noodles, poured with broth. The name of this dish is translated from Kyrgyz as "five fingers", and it is traditionally eaten with the fingers. The traditional soup "shorpo" is also popular among people. This is a hot broth with chunks of meat, potatoes, carrots and greens. The dish of fried meat is called "kuurdak": meat (lamb, beef or horse meat) is being cut into large pieces and fried with onions on the fat of tail. Horse meat sausage "chuchuk" and sausage from the liver and blood with spices "byzhy" are considered as real delicacy.

Dairy products also are an integral part of Kyrgyz people's meals. People like to drink ayran, very thick fermented beverage made from sheep's milk. The key to good health and longevity has always been drinking of "kumys", an extremely beneficial drink of fermented mare's milk prepared on the jailoo in summer. Traditional types of cheese "syuzmo" and "kurut" (solid small white balls with a salty taste) are also made from milk. Syuzmo can be diluted with water, then you'll get the best thirst-quenching beverage "chalap".

Traditional beverages are also made from millet and barley. Bozo is a national drink, similar to beer, which is made from millet, wheat or corn. Particularly popular summer drinks "djarma" and "maksym" are made from barley flour "talkan" in the process of fermentation.

No dinner is complete without bread. Usually it is round-shaped. It is baked in a cauldron (“kemkerme tokoch”), in a frying pan (“kemechten”) or in oven (“tandyr-nan”). On holidays people cook a special regale “boorsok”, fried sweet pieces of dough.

Every meal is accompanied by a cup of tea. People drink black and green tea, with milk, cream or melted butter. After a long journey tea perfectly quenches thirst, and after receiving high-calorie fatty foods tea is a real lifesaver for the body. Tea is usually drunk from a special bows pialas.

It’s also common for Kyrgyz families to cook dishes borrowed from other nations. These dishes refer to Dungan and Uighur cuisine. They are ashlyam fu and lagman (noodles with spicy sauce, meat and vegetables), manti and chuchvara (boiled dough stuffed with minced meat). Pilaf (a dish of rice, carrots and meat) came from Uzbek cuisine. It is usually cooked for holidays and festivities.

Ethno-games and competitions

National entertainment occupies a prominent place in the life of Kyrgyz people. Various ethno-games and competitions are extremely popular. They are also one of the most important elements of nomadic culture, as they helped to develop the necessary skills and qualities of nomads: riding skill, strength, agility, endurance and accuracy.

Falcon Hunting or Golden Eagle Hunting with golden eagles is an ancient tradition that originates from the 12th and 13th century, when a good golden eagle and a fast horse had the same value and gave their owner a noticeable authority.

Eagle hunter is called Berkutchi in local language. Despite the fact that, over time, this practice gradually disappeared, hunting with birds (especially with golden eagle) is still popular in Kyrgyzstan. Hunting takes place on a specially prepared horse. So that the rider had the opportunity to hold the golden eagle, a special "baldak" device was fitted to the saddle to support his hand.

Usually, they hunt for young deers, foxes, and other small animals. During the hunt, the golden eagle rushes down and kills them with lightning speed. Golden Eagles are even able to kill young wolves when they are not able to cope with deep snow. Sometimes golden eagles hunt in pairs, just like they would in the wild.

Eagle hunting has become part of World Nomad Games, which Kyrgyzstan initiated in 2014. Eagle hunters from all over the world come to Kyrgyzstan to compete in this sport. World Nomad Games are prototype of Olympic games, where sportsmen of nomadic disciplines gather to perform on international stage.

An experienced couple, a Berkutchi (a hunter) and a bird, can, on average, catch 50 or 60 foxes, a dozen badgers, a pair of lynxes and 4 - 5 wolves, for a normal four-month season that starts in late autumn.

Training of golden eagles takes a lot of time (3-4 years), it should be done by one person and the process requires constant daily attention. Most birds (with an average lifespan of 40 years) are caught young, they are dressed on their heads with a special hood and placed in a cage with a roost that constantly swings, while Berkuchi sings special songs to the bird so that the bird can get used to his voice. (Later, the golden eagle will be able to discern human voices and will only respond to the call of his master). Berkutchi feeds the bird himself.

When the golden eagle has almost reached adulthood, the owner shows him the skin and fur of those animals that he has to hunt for, so that he is accustomed to the smell and characteristics of prey. All this is done with the help of special commands. Training continues by dragging the fox fur behind the galloping horse. Not all Golden Eagles are suitable for training, but only those that have a special devotion.

Demonstration of eagle hunting can be performed all year round as part of tours for cultural learning and exchange.

Arts and Crafts of Kyrgyz People

Arts and crafts of Kyrgyz people has evolved over the centuries. It was formed based on the needs of people's everyday life, and the nomadic way of life influenced it much. Among the major forms of arts and crafts felt art, weaving, patterned embroidery, making of mat, leather products, jewellery, and wood carving.

The art of making felt products is closely related to the dwelling of the nomads, the yurt. Carpets of felt, decorated with ornaments, are called "shyrdaks". Shyrdak is a very important element in the decoration of a yurt. It is usually located on the floor. Felts for shyrdaks are made from sheep wool, which is tightly rolled and painted in bright colors. Felt is made from pieces of ornament, then they are sewn together to form a beautiful carpet. Shyrdak's length is usually four meters. width is about two meters. The great meaning in the applied arts has the carpet "ala kiyiz" (kyrg.

"motley felt"). It differs from shyrdak that felt pieces are not sewn, but they are rolled to each other.

The art of making mats is also popular among craftsmen. Mats are made from woven straw called "chiy" and threads of colored wool. The mats are widely used in everyday life. They are important components of the yurt, and they are layed under felt carpets to protect them from moisture.

Embroidery also can be noted as significant craft of Kyrgyz people. Often only women involved in it. They skillfully embroider patterns and ornaments on fabrics, leather and felt. Kyrgyz masters magnificently embroider wall pictures "tush-kiyiz". Such pictures' center is usually plain, without patterns, while the sides are framed by the wonderful color ornaments. Pattern embroidery is also common for traditional bags "ayak-kap" and hanging shelves "tekche".

Leather products made by local artisans can be noted as unique items. They are not just clothes and shoes, but also vessels ("sabaa", "chanach", "kookor"), framing for chests, cases and horse equipment.

Wooden products are made of different tupes, for example, elm, juniper, poplar and cherry trees. These products are dinnerware, chests and boxes, racks and cases, special chess and backgammon, musical instruments.

The skills of goldsmiths called "zerger-usta" are highly appreciated. For Kyrgyz people silver metal is sacred, it is not only a decoration, but also a ward off for evil spirits. Silver rings ("shakek"), bracelets ("bilerik"), pectorals ("soyko", "jel-byurooch"), silver decoration for braids ("chach ushtuk") are extremely popular among Kyrgyz women.

You can get acquainted with Kyrgyz arts and crafts and even purchase some of the items in many towns and villages by visiting handicraft centers, workshops, exhibitions or special shops.

Beaitiful Sceneries and Places of Kyrgyzstan

Magnificent Tien Shan and Pamir-Alai Mountain ranges covers more than 90% of its area, featuring the extremely high mountains Pobeda Peak (7,439m), Lenin Peak (7,134m) and Khan-Tengri Peak (7,010m). It is the home for the lovers of mountaineering, trekking, downhill skiing, snowboarding and other adventure tourism activities.

Mountains and valleys are the main components of the relief of Kyrgyzstan. On their tops there are more than 8,000 glaciers which are important sources of fresh water. In Kyrgyzstan there are two massive mountain ranges: the Tien-Shan and Pamir-Alai.

Pobeda Peak is the highest mountain peak in Kyrgyzstan. It is located in the mountains of the Tien Shan Mountain range to the east of Issyk-Kul Lake, closer to the Kyrgyz-Chinese border. Pobeda Peak, like Lenin Peak, is among the top five seven thousand meters high peaks of the country. Its height is 7439 meters above sea level. The peak was not conquered until 1956.

The height of Lenin Peak is 7134 meters above sea level. The mountain peak is located on Chon-Alai Range, located between Kyrgyzstan and Tajikistan. For the first time Lenin Peak was conquered in 1928.

Khan-Tengri Peak or known in circles of climbers, as "Lord of the Sky" is located on Tengri-Tag ridge, located on the border of Kazakhstan, China and Kyrgyzstan. Its height is 7010 meters above sea level.

The peak of Military Topographers, 6873 meters high above sea level, is located in the Central Tien Shan on the Muztag massif.

The next three peaks are located in the same area, but slightly inferior in height to "Military Topographer". Thus, in the upper reaches of the Southern Inylchek glacier, there is a series of well-known six thousand meters: the Peak of Friendship (6,800 meters), the Peak of Shater (6,700 meters) and the Peak of Chapaev (6,371 meters).

The Abshir-Say tract is a picturesque canyon-shaped gorge. It is located seventy kilometres from the city of Osh.

The bottom of the gorge lies at an altitude of 1500 to 2500 meters above sea level. The picturesque canyon formed by the river of the same name, framed by sheer cliffs, is a unique monument of nature. The flow here is quite turbulent and the waterfalls of this river is an impressive sight. The waters of the Abshir-Say River have healing properties. Ephemeral plants grow here, archa. Translated from the Tajik, the name of the tract means water-milk source.

Borders with two neighbouring countries such as Tajikistan and Uzbekistan are located in Fergana Valley. That makes it ethnically diverse places in Central Asia. Naryn and Kara-Dariya rivers merge in the valley forming Syrdarya river. Traveling around the valley maybe sometimes challenging due to border disputes. Main occupation of people living in the region is agriculture and animal husbandry. Border bazaars and natural beauty of the valley attract plenty of tourists.

Chuy Valley is lies between two countries: in the South of Kazakhstan and in the North of Kyrgyzstan. The capital of Kyrgyzstan is located in Chuy Valley, the region is called Chuy oblast, which is the most populated region of the country. Popular destinations in the valley are Ala-Archa National Park and The Burana Tower.

Suusamyr Valley is high attitude valley located 130 from Bishkek between Kyrgyz Ala-Too, Kyrgyz Ala-Tau and Jumgal-Too ridge forming a triangle with longest side 100 km. Its highest point reaches 4500 meters. The road from Bishkek to Suusamyr lies among picturesque

Too-Ashu Gorge. Thanks to abundant snowfalls, unique alpine conditions, constant low temperature with dry air and no wind, its unique "Tien-Shan" snow is formed here - dry and crumbly, making Suusamyr unique for skiing snowboarding, heli-ski, and backcountry. There are two ski resorts Suusamyr and Too-Ashu, which attract winter sports lovers from December to April. During spring and summer, visitors come for hiking, camping, and kymyz treatment.

Arpa Valley is fairly long and located in the south of Naryn Region. Its dimensions are 60 to 32 km. From all sides the valley is surrounded by mountain ranges: the Fergana, Torugart, At-Bashinsky ranges, as well as the Ortok-Too and Jaman-Too ranges.

Arpa Valley is located at an altitude of more than 2,900 meters above sea level. The climate here is rather severe: winters are cold and summers are warm but short. The height of snow cover can exceed 60 sm. Meadows of the valley are used as pastures for cattle.

Alay Valley (locals call it simply Alay) is a stunningly picturesque part of the Pamir-Alay, a tectonic cavity located between the Alay and Zaalai ranges in southern Kyrgyzstan at altitudes of 2240 - 3536 meters. The valley extends from west to east for 150 km from 8 up to 25 km. The Alai Range is inferior in height to Zaalai, hiding greeny summer pastures (jailoo) in its gorges. Ever-white peaks of Alay Range are high, massive, but reaching to the sky and sun.

Previously, a section of the caravan road of the famous Great Silk Road went through Torugart Pass (3752 meters). Today high-altitude Pamir Road - its section Osh - Khorog, goes through the eastern part of the valley.

Protected Objects of Nature help to preserve the unique natural landscapes of Kyrgyzstan in their original form. In order to save wonderful natural landscapes, flora and fauna of the country there were created 6 reserves, 2 biosphere reserves protected by UNESCO and 75 national parks.

Ala-Archa National Park

Ala-Archa gorge is one of the most famous sights of Kyrgyzstan. The Ala-Archa gorge is located in the Chuy Region, and is a national park. Every year, this alpine gorge receives hundreds of thousands of tourists, both local and foreign. There are several reasons for this popularity. Firstly, the Ala-Archa gorge is located only 30 kilometers from Bishkek and therefore it is very easy to get here and there is all the necessary tourist infrastructure: a good asphalt road, shops, hotels, cafes, and places to relax among beautiful nature. Secondly, the Ala-Archa gorge has its own geographical features - it is located on the central and highest part of the Kyrgyz ridge - the second longest Tien Shan ridge. Therefore, it is there where the mountains rise as high as possible above the plain, where numerous trails begin to the highest peaks of the Kyrgyz ridge. Ala-Archa is famous for its untouched nature: vast spruce forests, birch groves, numerous springs with clear glacial water and mighty cliffs.

Walnut and fruit forests of Arslanbob

Arslanbob Forest (also Arstanbap) is a large walnut forest located in the mountains of Ferghana and Chatkal ranges, in Jalal-Abad Region, at an altitude of 1700 meters. This is the largest walnut forest in the world and one of the most amazing places in Kyrgyzstan. Arslanbob forest is a natural forest that arose in ancient times.

Scientists claim that his age may exceed 50 million years. The area of Arslanbob is 700,000 hectares, and numerous walnuts, pistachio, almond, cherry plum, pear and many others grow on this vast territory. The total number of plants growing here exceeds 130. But anyway, the most noticeable part of the forest is walnut trees. The age of individual trees exceeds 1000 years, and each of them brings from 150 to 400 kilograms of nuts every year. In addition to the forest itself, the area around is very remarkable. The slopes of the Ferghana and Chatkal ranges in this place are composed of dolomite, and therefore are very different from other Tien Shan mountains in their unusual color and relief. The mighty white cliffs are adjacent to the endless green expanses of the Arslanbob forest, making this place absolutely unique. Such a large forest requires a large amount of water, and therefore this region is rich in numerous streams and rivers. There are also several waterfalls, the most notable of which are Big Arslanbob (80 meters) and Small Arslanbob (35 meters). Also on the territory of the reserve there are several lakes, one of which is sacred and called Kel-Mazar. Towering at this place, Babash-Ata peak, 4,436 meters high, is also considered sacred among the inhabitants of this place.

Sarychat-Ertash Reserve

Sarychat-Ertash State Reserve is quite young from the reserves of Kyrgyzstan. This is a specially protected natural area, formed in 1995, which is located in Issyk-Kul region.

It was organized by Decree of the Government of the Kyrgyz Republic and is included as a core zone in the Issyk-Kul Biosphere Territory, the status of the reserve in the World Network of Bioreserves (UNESCO 2002) in order to preserve unique natural complexes, rare and endangered species of animals and plants in Issyk-Kul region, as well as maintaining the overall ecological balance of the region. The territory of the reserve is located at the junction of Inner and Central Tien Shan in Sarychat-Ertash-Uchkul valley (a tributary of Sary-Jaz River) and is a site typical of a high-altitude zone. The total area of the reserve is 135,4 thousand ha, of which 72,080 thousand ha are allocated to the core zone, and 62,060 thousand ha to the buffer zone, located at altitudes from 2000 to 5000 meters above sea level.

Sary-Chelek Reserve

Sary-Chelek Reserve is located in the western part of the Jalal-Abad Region, in the foothills of the Chatkal Range, at an altitude of 1940 meters. It includes a mountain called Sary-Chelek Lake, the largest in Western Tien-Shan and is the basis of the reserve and overall, there are five lakes. The largest of the other lakes in this area are Iri-Kel and Kyla-Kel lakes, which are inferior in size to Sary-Chelek Lake, but not at all inferior in beauty. Due to the depth not as deep as in Sary-Chelek itself, at the bottom of these small lakes you can clearly see trunks of fallen trees and see flocks of frightened fish. The territory of Sary-Chelek biosphere reserve begins on the southern shore of the lake, which was created to preserve the unique natural diversity of this area. Within the reserve there is a large forest land consisting of walnut and fruit trees. Around Sary-Chelek Reserve there are winding hiking trails for trekking and horseback riding pass, leading to the shores of five Sary-Chelek lakes through small but rather steep passes. The tourist base of the lake is the village of Arkyt, located a few kilometers below the lake Sary-Chelek. Also on Sary-Chelek Lake you can ride a motor boat to see the far part of the lake, which is almost invisible from the shore.

Chon-Kemin National Park

Chon-Kemin National Park is an environmental, research institution, and belongs to the category of specially protected natural areas of the Kyrgyz Republic. It was formed in 1997 in order to preserve natural complexes, forests, fauna and flora, which have special environmental, aesthetic value, due to the favorable combination of natural and cultural landscapes, and for use in recreational, educational, scientific and as cultural center. The climate of the region is sharply continental with great diversity depending on the height above sea level, exposure and slope steepness. At equal heights, the northern slopes are colder and wetter, the southern slopes are warmer and drier. In the zone where the settlements of the valley are located, the average temperature in January is –10.5 °C, and in July –17.0 °C. In the reserve Chon-Kemin River flows from northeast to south-west between western halves of these ranges. Its length is about 120 km. Chon-Kemin Reserve also has two small alpine lakes. The moraine-dammed Dzhashyl-Kol (Chelek) Lake is located at an altitude from 3150 to 3427 meters above sea level. Köl-Tör (Kel - Kogur Lake) is located at an altitude from 2420 to 2465 meters above sea level on the northern slope of the Kungei-Ala-Too ridge. The area of the lake is about 16 hectares.

Lakes in Kyrgyzstan

There are more than 2000 high-altitude lakes nestled and Issyk-Kul is the world's second largest crater-lake in the northeast with a surface area of 6 236 km2. **Lake Issyk-Kul** is considered **one of the largest mountain lakes in the world.** Both the southern and northern shores of Issyk-Kul are different from each other with Skazka canyons, Barskoon and Dzhety-Oguz gorges and the best beaches and sun. **Swimming in the Issyk-Kul Lake** is a pleasure, because the water in it is crystal clear and warm.

One of the highlights of the must visit is the lake Son-Kul, located at an altitude of 3016 meters. Here you have a unique opportunity to sleep in a yurt, experience the nomadic lifestyle and ride horses.

10 reasons to visit Kyrgyzstan

Kyrgyzstan is an amazing country in **Central Asia**, folk customs are very simple here, and residents of most regions still lead a nomadic lifestyle for almost a thousand years.

Large expanses of Kyrgyzstan and its small population can give a tourist a lot of impressions. Kyrgyzstan is famous for its large **alpine lakes,** whose height does not fall below 3000 meters, as well as for its numerous beautiful and difficult passes.

1. **Celestial mountains and adventure tours:** Kyrgyzstan is home to the magnificent Tien Shan and

Pamir-Alai Mountain ranges. Kyrgyzstan is a good place for fans of active sports like hiking, trekking, cycling, horse riding, because almost 90 percent of Kyrgyzstan is covered with mountains.

2. **Fresh air and virgin nature in Kyrgyzstan:** Mountains, gorges, magnificent passes, canyons, and valleys. Kyrgyzstan has a huge number of mesmerizing views that make you fall in love with this landscape. The world-famous Issyk Kul Lake, also known as the "Pearl of Central Asia", is located here.

3. **Winter tourism:** Staying in Kyrgyzstan is a great opportunity to go for skiing or snowboarding. Sky resorts in Kyrgyzstan are quite diverse. Many facilities have routes of varying difficulty, equipment rentals and experienced instructors.

4. **Culture of nationalities in Kyrgyzstan — history, people, clothing:** Kyrgyzstan is considered a multi-ethnic country; in Kyrgyzstan you will have more opportunities to learn about the customs and traditions of other nationalities.

5. **Hospitality in Kyrgyzstan:** The people in Kyrgyzstan are very hospitable, kind and open. Guests have always been welcome and honoured among the Kyrgyz people, don't be surprised if at the first meeting you were invited to visit someone's home, because this is the whole aesthetics of the Kyrgyz people.

6. **Traditional famous Kyrgyz meal:** Kyrgyz honey, «**besh barmak**», «pilaf», «samsa», «manty», «nan», **kurut**», fruits and drinks such as «chalap», "**kymys**» will make any tourist remember Kyrgyzstan for a long time.

7. **Nomadic lifestyle and culture:** Kyrgyzstan has a rich nomadic heritage and traditions that have been woven into the identity of the Kyrgyz people. Despite the fact that the Kyrgyz were considered a nomadic people 100 years ago, nowadays population also lead a nomadic lifestyle. Every summer most of the population go to «Jailoo», where they get to stay in the «yurt» and enjoy drink «kymys».

8. **The Great Silk Road:** The Great Silk Road. Caravanserai. The Pamir Highway. For two millennia, the Great Silk Road was the key trade route linking the pinnacles of eastern and western civilization. Caravans, laden with people and goods, crossed mountains, deserts. Rivers and continents, spreading ideas, technologies, religions and wealth to peoples and culture along their path. Kyrgyzstan has a huge number of ancient petroglyphs of great archaeological value, some of which date back to the Late Bronze Age, around 1500 BC, and most of them date back to the period from the 1st to the 8th century AD.

9. **Vacation without social media:** Many people nowadays spend most of their time on the Internet and on social media. Your stay in the Kyrgyz Mountain will quickly solve this problem. Since you won't be able to use the internet, your only reason to take out your phone is to take pictures of the landscape and your friends.

10. **Convenient movement:** In Kyrgyzstan, you do not need to look for a taxi, because here the taxi drivers are looking for you, the tourist only needs to get to the station. One of the most important is that there is no timetable for public transport in Kyrgyzstan.